The Weight Of Unsaid Words

Poetic Musings on Love, Society and the Battles Within

Yadi Baber

Dedication

To Papa, Mumma, Yatharth and Sky,
You are the foundation of my world, the steady hands that have held me through storms, and the quiet strength that has taught me resilience. Your love, sacrifices, and unspoken words have shaped me in more ways than I can express.

To everyone who has been a part of my life—those who stayed, those who left, and those who changed me along the way—this book carries pieces of you. Your stories, your struggles, your moments of silence and strength have found a home in these pages.

This book is for all the emotions we often leave unspoken.

Preface

Words have a way of staying with us, especially the ones left unsaid. They linger in the spaces between conversations, in the glances that hold more than spoken language ever could, in the weight of memories we carry but never share.

The Weight of Unsaid Words is a collection of those emotions—some personal, some drawn from the lives around me, and many that I believe will resonate with you. It speaks of love and loss, resilience and regret, fleeting moments and lifelong wounds. It is a mirror to the experiences we all navigate in different ways, yet feel so deeply.

I have always believed that poetry is more than just words; it is a reflection of life itself. Each poem in this book is a moment captured, a feeling acknowledged, a story that deserved to be told. Some might remind you of a person, a time, or a part of yourself you've long tucked away. Others may simply give you the comfort of knowing that you are not alone in your thoughts.

This book is not about answers, nor is it about closure. It is about feeling, about remembering, about finding solace in knowing that even in silence, we are understood.

And so, I invite you to read, to reflect, and perhaps, to find the courage to say the words you've kept inside for too long.

Acknowledgements

Writing this book has been an emotional journey, one that would not have been possible without the moments, people, and experiences that shaped it. While the poems are mine, the emotions behind them belong to all of us— to the heartbreaks we endure, the battles we fight in silence, and the love we give without expecting anything in return.

To those who have shared their stories with me, knowingly or unknowingly, thank you. To those who have been a source of inspiration—through kindness, through pain, through their presence or absence—this book carries pieces of you.

And to the readers who will find their own reflections in these pages, thank you for allowing my words to become a part of your journey.

This book is for you.

1. My First Love

You stepped into motherhood far too soon,
With dreams still young beneath the moon.
Yet when the world gave you no space,
You built a home with love and grace.

With empty hands but a heart so wide,
You worked through nights and never cried.
A single parent, yet never alone,
For every struggle, you faced on your own.

You woke before the sun each day,
Yet never let me see your fray.
Between my books and your endless calls,
You stood unshaken through it all.

When we had nothing, you still gave,
So I could learn, so I'd be brave.
I've never said these words out loud,
But, Mom, you make me strong and proud.

You hid your pain behind a smile,
Walked weary miles, yet stayed awhile.
You'd mend my world when it fell apart,
Yet stitched your own with a breaking heart.

You missed the meals so I could eat,
You stitched my clothes, kept my shoes neat.
You never asked for more than love,
Yet gave me more than enough.

Through every scar, through every ache,
You carried burdens for my sake.
Yet even in your silent fight,
You held my hand and showed me light.

You are my heart, my strength, my home,
The purest love I've ever known.
No words could ever quite convey,
But, Maa, I love you more each day.

"A mother's love is the first love we ever know—pure, unbreakable, given without conditions. She gives, and gives, and gives, until there is almost nothing left, yet she never asks for anything in return. This poem is a tribute to the silent sacrifices, the quiet strength, and the unwavering love of every mother who put her child before herself."

2. I Still Look for You

I lost you too soon, but never in heart,
Your absence rips my world apart.
I search for you in every place,
In fading dreams, in time's embrace.

You gave your all, yet took so little,
Your hands were worn, your love was brittle.
You stood behind, so we could rise,
A silent hero in disguise.

I still hear your voice from long ago,
"Let them talk, just let it go."
"Study hard, be kind, stay true—
One day, the world will bow to you."

You never let me feel alone,
You were my spine, my flesh, my bone.
My biggest fan, my guiding light,
The one who made my wrongs feel right.

But fate was cruel, it took you fast,
And left a void too deep, too vast.
I miss you, Papa, every day,
In uncried tears and words I pray.

If love could bring the lost ones near,
You'd be right here, you'd still be here.

"Some goodbyes are never truly final. People fade from our lives, but not from our thoughts. We carry them in the spaces they once filled, in the habits they left behind, in the quiet moments where we still catch ourselves searching. Perhaps we're not looking for them—just for the feeling we lost when they left."

3. Lost Love

I traced your name in empty air,
A whisper left, but you weren't there.
The echoes hum where laughter grew,
Now silence lingers—cold and true.

I reach for hands that slip through time,
For voices lost, for love once mine.
Yet memories dance in faded hues,
Like autumn leaves in morning's dew.

I walk the streets we used to roam,
Where every step still feels like home.
Yet home's an echo, not a place,
A hollow ache I can't erase.

The nights once filled with endless calls,
Now stretch too long, an empty sprawl.
I still press send, though I know well,
Your name won't light my screen to tell.

I pass by cafés, the corner seat,
Where our old ghosts still tend to meet.
I sit alone, but in my mind,
You're laughing there, just killing time.

Some loves don't die, they just grow quiet,
They live in dreams we can't rewrite.
In all the words we left unsaid,
And all the tears we never shed.

So here I stand where endings start,
A love once held now torn apart.
Yet still, it lingers, soft but true—
A part of me, a piece of you.

"Some loves don't truly disappear; they just settle into the quiet corners of our hearts. It's not the goodbye that lingers, but the echoes of what once was—the places, the memories, the habits that refuse to fade. And maybe, that's how love stays, not in presence, but in the spaces it once filled."

4. Not Lonely, Just Brave

They ask me if the silence weighs me down,
If the empty seats and quiet nights make me frown.
But I have found a rhythm in my own heartbeat,
A symphony in the sound of my steady feet.

They call it loneliness, but I call it peace,
A world without chaos, a soul at ease.
No forced smiles, no borrowed words,
Just the comfort of thoughts left undisturbed.

I walk alone, but I do not stray,
For the path is mine in every way.
No footsteps to follow, no voices to guide,
Only my own, walking side by side.

The world believes in crowded rooms,
In laughter that echoes, in love that looms.
But joy is not measured in numbers or noise,
It is found in the quiet, in self-made joys.

I've heard them whisper, "You must be sad,"
As if solitude is something bad.
Yet, they never see the strength it takes,
To be your own anchor when the whole world shakes.

It takes courage to stand where no one stays,
To find warmth in cold and light in grays.
To embrace yourself without disguise,
To look in the mirror and recognize—

That I am whole, though I stand apart,
Loneliness is a stranger to my heart.
For in the stillness, I've come alive,
Not lonely, just brave enough to thrive.

"Being alone is often misunderstood—it is not a wound, but a choice, a state of being where one finds strength in their own presence. It takes courage to walk paths where no one joins, to seek comfort in solitude when the world glorifies crowds. But solitude isn't emptiness; it's a quiet freedom, a place where true strength is nurtured."

5. A Home Too Far

I've drifted too far from the place I belong,
Where laughter once echoed, so pure, so strong.
No eager voices ask me now,
"When will you come? Are you home somehow?"

Festivals pass like fleeting dreams,
Seen through screens in pixel streams.
A hug replaced by a frozen frame,
FaceTime dinners just aren't the same.

The scent of home, the evening chai,
Maa's warm touch, her soft lullaby.
No five-star meal, no grand buffet,
Can match the taste of her hands that day.

I prayed to grow, to break away,
When school felt like a heavy chain each day.
Now I crave those endless nights,
Of silly fights and childhood sights.

Freedom was sweet, but no one said,
It comes with a silence I now dread.
I'm happy, I am, but just so you know—
Some nights, I still long for home's warm glow.

"Home is more than a place—it's a feeling, a belonging, a warmth that isn't always found in four walls. Sometimes, no matter how far we travel or how long we stay, home remains a memory, a longing, a destination we may never quite reach."

6. Unbreakable Bond

Through storms and fire, we stand as one,
From childhood battles to laughter spun.
The TV remote, a daily war,
Ice cream split right to the core.

We fought for toys, we fought for space,
We fought like rivals in a race.
From stolen pens to hiding shoes,
Every day brought brand-new feuds.

I swore I hated you, so did you,
Yet somehow, love still pushed us through.
Mom made me take you to my friend's birthday,
I rolled my eyes, but you still stayed.

Back then, we swore we'd never be close,
Yet here we are, who would've known?
Now grown up, all wise and smart,
But still connected, heart to heart.

You know my highs, you see my lows,
Like a mirror, you just know.
You track my flights, you check my way,
You call to ask, "Where did you go today?"

You show up early, rain or shine,
At every airport, every time.
We fight, we bicker, we drive insane,
Yet love still lingers, unchanged, untamed.

Through silent tears and endless cheers,
Through all the reckless, stubborn years,
One thing's sure, come what may,
You're stuck with me, forever to stay.

"Some connections defy time, distance, and even conflict. They bend but never break, held together by an unspoken understanding, a love that needs no validation. True bonds aren't measured by how often you speak but by how deeply you're felt, even in silence."

7. The Beauty in Broken

The cracks within still glow with gold,
A story of pain, yet beauty untold.
Not just of love that slipped away,
But silent aches we hide each day.

The friend who left without a trace,
The love that time could not replace.
The words unsaid, the calls ignored,
The quiet wars we've all endured.

The weight of being second choice,
The unheard scream behind the voice.
The loss of dreams, the fading light,
The wounds we bandage out of sight.

But every scar and shattered part,
Still beats within a fearless heart.
For even when the world feels cold,
The cracks within still glow with gold.

"We often hide our scars, thinking they make us less, but they are the very proof of our survival. There is beauty in the cracks, in the pieces we've put back together with resilience and grace. Broken does not mean ruined—it means we have lived, we have endured, and we have found strength where we never thought to look."

8. The Night Was Long, But Dawn Still Came

The night was long, the weight was deep,
A silent war I dared not speak.
For in a world that shut its ears,
My pain was met with doubts, not tears.

"It's all in your head," they used to say,
"Be strong, just pray, it'll go away."
But prayers don't quiet the thoughts that scream,
Or wake you up from a hollow dream.

I smiled, I laughed, I played my part,
While darkness gnawed inside my heart.
Too scared to say, too tired to fight,
Would they call me broken if they knew my plight?

I whispered my pain, but no one heard,
So I buried it deep beneath my words.
I feared their stares, their judging minds,
Would they see my wounds or just read the lines?

But pain ignored still finds a way,
To steal the light, to dim the day.
I couldn't sleep, I couldn't breathe,
Trapped beneath what they couldn't see.

And then one day, I broke, I bled,
I chose to fight instead of pretend.
A hand reached out, a voice so kind,
A lifeline in a world so blind.

Therapists, pills, a helping hand,
A path to walk, a place to stand.
Not weakness, shame, nor silent blame,
Just healing slow, just calling my name.

So if you're drowning, lost in pain,
If every day just feels the same,
Hold on, my love, don't be ashamed,
The night was long, but dawn still came.

"Pain can feel endless, and darkness can seem absolute. But time has a way of turning even the longest night into morning. No matter how heavy the sorrow, how deep the despair—light always finds a way back. And when it does, you realize that surviving was the bravest thing you ever did."

9. The Friends I Found, The Friends I Lost

I met my first friend when I was small,
Hand in hand, we had it all.
Tea parties, dolls, secret plans,
Laughter echoing through our hands.

Then school began, the world grew wide,
A friend who stayed right by my side.
Waited for her bus before the bell,
Holding my hand when I didn't feel well.

Then came another, fierce and bold,
We whispered stories never told.
Passing notes, stealing time,
Swearing "forever" in inked-up lines.

College arrived, and so did them,
A wild soul who made me fam.
Dancing barefoot in the rain,
Drunk on dreams, numb to pain.

Then life got fast, work took hold,
I met friends with a heart of gold.
Shared coffee, breakdowns, midnight calls,
Holding each other through the falls.

And somewhere else, in places unknown,
A stranger became the safest home.
Not childhood, not school, not work nor play,
Yet the one who never walked away.

We laughed, we cried, we swore we'd stay,
But life has a way of drifting away.
Different cities, different lands,
Conversations slipping through our hands.

Now, messages fade, the calls run dry,
Yet some nights, I sit and sigh.
Scrolling through memories, lost in the past,
Wishing I'd known those days wouldn't last.

So if you have a friend you miss,
Send that text, don't wait for this.
For friendships fade, but love remains,
And time won't give us back these days.

"Friendships are chapters, some lasting a lifetime, others

closing too soon. People come and go, leaving imprints on our hearts, shaping the people we become. Losing friends is painful, but finding the right ones is a gift. In the end, it's not about how many stayed but about the ones who truly mattered."

10. Smiling Through the Screens

I walked in fresh, my hopes held high,
A suit, a dream, a suit-and-tie.
The world was mine, or so I thought,
A place where talent could not be bought.

The team was warm, the air felt light,
Lunch breaks filled with jokes so bright.
Managers spoke of goals so grand,
Promotions promised, hand in hand.

But years passed by, the weight grew deep,
Late-night calls stole hours of sleep.
Emails at dawn, deadlines tight,
No time to pause, no end in sight.

The meetings drained, the voices loud,
Yet no one dared to call it out.
A cycle spun of silent fears,
A future blurred with unpaid tears.

The ladder climbed, yet stayed the same,
Favoritism played the game.
The work was mine, the credit theirs,
The ceiling high, the heart in prayers.

Layoffs came like waves of doubt,
No warning signs, just names crossed out.
Would I survive? Or would I fall?
Tomorrow's fate—a coin's recall.

Yet still I smile, I nod, I cheer,
A corporate face, my mask so clear.
For if I break or speak my mind,
They'll find a way to leave me behind.

So I endure, I play my part,
A worker's mind, a dreamer's heart.
For someday soon, I'll break these chains,
And find myself beyond the pain.

"Corporate life often demands more than just work—it demands a piece of you. It's a world where effort isn't always rewarded, where voices get lost in the noise of deadlines, and where loyalty is a currency that doesn't always pay back. This poem speaks for the countless professionals who put on a brave face, even when the

weight of unspoken exhaustion sits heavy on their shoulders. But beyond the grind, there is always a way out, a chance to reclaim yourself before the system takes too much."

11. The Love That Broke Me

It started with warmth, a golden embrace,
A love so fierce, a perfect place.
"You're the best thing that's happened to me," you'd say,
And I drank it in, swept away.

Days were drenched in flowers and light,
Every word you spoke felt right.
You held my hand, you read my mind,
Told me "You're rare, you're one of a kind."

But love like that was never free,
The tides soon turned, crashing on me.
Your smile faded, the air ran cold,
The fairytale cracked, the lies took hold.

"You're too much, too sensitive, never enough,"
Your voice was sweet, but your touch grew rough.
Your mistakes were mine, your guilt my load,
I wore the blame like a heavy coat.

The silence cut sharper than words could bite,
Then came the storms, the endless fights.
Gaslit into doubt, I questioned my mind,
"Maybe I am broken," maybe you were right.

Apologies whispered, then erased overnight,
Sweetness returned, but it never felt right.
I clung to hope, to the love I once knew,
But love should never leave bruises in blue.

I stayed too long, out of fear, out of shame,
Felt the weight of the words, the burns of my name.
Until one day, the mirror screamed back,
"You are fading, slipping through the cracks."

The bruises spoke what my lips never said,
The tears stained pillows where nightmares bred.
But hands reached out—friends, family, a guide,
Pulled me back from the war inside.

Now, the nights still whisper, the shadows still creep,
But I'm standing tall, no longer weak.
I've stitched my scars, I've found my ground,
The love that broke me will never be found.

*"Not all love stories end with warmth. Some leave behind
scars, unanswered questions, and a version of us we no*

longer recognize. But even the love that breaks us teaches us something—it shows us our strength, our resilience, and our ability to heal. This poem is for those who have walked away, not because they stopped loving, but because they started choosing themselves."

12. Tides and Time

I sink my feet into the cooling sand,
The ocean hums, the waves expand.
A restless tide, a rhythmic beat,
Like echoes of the past, bittersweet.

Thirty years have come and gone,
Some I conquered, some felt wrong.
Dreams once bright as the morning sun,
Faded, shifted—lost or won?

I think of love that slipped away,
Of hands I held, yet couldn't stay.
Of words I spoke, of those I swallowed,
Of roads I chose, of dreams left hollowed.

The ocean moves, yet stays the same,
A lesson wrapped in salt and rain.
We chase, we crave, we rise, we fall,
Yet time moves on—despite it all.

I wonder if the younger me,
Would smile or sigh at who they see.
Would they scold me for the chances missed?
Or whisper, "You were meant for this."

The sky dims soft in amber hues,
Like fleeting days I didn't choose.
Some roads I walked, some left behind,
Yet all have shaped this heart, this mind.

So I sit and watch the waves return,
Some lessons heal, some lessons burn.
I may not have it figured out,
But I have today—that much, no doubt.

"Life moves like the tide—sometimes pulling us toward dreams, other times washing them away. Looking back, we often wonder about the roads we didn't take, the chances we missed, the versions of ourselves that could have been. But every wave that recedes makes space for a new one. This poem is a reminder that no matter where we stand today, we are still moving, still learning, and still becoming."

13. For Nani, The Words I Never Said

I never told you how much you mean,
How your love still lingers, soft yet unseen.
How your voice, a lullaby, calm and true,
Could turn my greyest skies to blue.

Summers smelled of mango and spice,
Of stolen sweets and scoldings twice.
You'd chase me down with a loving glare,
"Eat some more—don't leave your chair!"

Your hands, so wrinkled, strong, yet kind,
Braiding my hair, shaping my mind.
Stories whispered in the evening glow,
Of days you lived, of things I'd know.

You stitched my sweaters, patched my fall,
Never tired, never stalled.
A silent shield through joy and ache,
A love too vast for words to take.

And yet, I rushed—I grew, I ran,
Life pulled me far from where it began.
Calls grew shorter, visits rare,
But you still asked, "Are you eating there?"

Now I sit by your side, words stuck inside,
A lifetime of love I let slide.
How do I tell you what you should know?
That you were my first home, my safest glow.

I press your hand, soft yet worn,
A touch that feels like coming home.
I search for words, but none feel right,
So I just hold on—just a little tight.

You smile at me, as if you knew,
That love was spoken in all we do.
No grand confessions, no perfect lines,
Just moments lived—forever mine.

"Love is often felt in the smallest gestures—braiding hair, saving the last sweet, a simple touch on the shoulder. Yet, we only realize the depth of these moments when they start slipping away. This poem is for all the unspoken words, the gratitude we meant to express but never did. Maybe love isn't always in the words—it's in

the memories, the quiet care, the understanding that lingers long after they're gone."

14. More Than a Pet, My Whole World

I plan my days around your needs, your meals, your
walks, your play,
Cancel outings, shift my plans—"Sorry, can't, I can't stay
away."
I take you places where I know you'll be welcome and
free,
And if they say "No pets allowed," then that place isn't
for me.

Your bed is the couch, my bed is yours—no debate, no
fight,
Because how could I ever say no when you curl up just
right?
I leave home and wonder—are you waiting by the door?
Are you pacing, are you lonely? Do you miss me even
more?

I check the cameras, send a treat, rush back sooner than I
said,

Because no party, no dinner, feels right with you alone
instead.
And when someone says, "It's just a pet," I feel a spark
ignite,
Because love like this, so pure, so true, could never be so
slight.

I see you tilt your head, eyes filled with something deep,
A knowing gaze, a silent bond, a promise we both keep.
You're not just a pet, you're the rhythm in my days,
The laughter in my silence, the warmth in all my ways.

If they don't get it, they never will—some hearts just
aren't built to see,
That you're not just a pet, my love, you are family to me.

*"Some bonds don't need words—they exist in shared
silences, in the wag of a tail, in the comforting weight of
a paw on your lap. To those who have loved and lost a
pet, the grief is just as real, just as heavy. Because they
were never just pets—they were family, they were home,
they were love in its purest form."*

15. Unseen Scars, Unheard Screams

A walk too fast, a glance too long,
A comment tossed where it doesn't belong.
A whistle cuts through the summer heat,
Unwanted eyes tracing my feet.

"Too dark, too pale, too fat, too thin,"
Judged by skin before I begin.
A laugh behind me, a muttered phrase,
Like acid burning through the haze.

A stranger's hand brushed where it shouldn't,
I froze in place, but scream—I couldn't.
On crowded streets, in empty lanes,
Their stares still crawl beneath my veins.

"Smile a little," they say to me,
As if my silence is their plea.
But every look, each sneering call,
Steals a piece—a wound too small.

I tug my top, I change my pace,
I hide my form, I mask my face.
Yet shame is theirs, not mine to bear,
So why's it me who walks in fear?

But no—no more will I walk and bend,
No more pretend, no more defend.
Their words, their laughs, their hands, their gaze,
Will never set my world ablaze.

For every time they tried to break,
I found the strength they couldn't take.
Not just a body, not just a name,
I am a fire they'll never tame.

"Not all wounds bleed. Some are carried in silence, buried beneath forced smiles and unspoken pain. We walk among people who carry invisible battles, scars that don't show but weigh just the same. This poem is for those who suffer quietly, for those who have learned to scream without making a sound. You are not alone. Your pain is real, and so is your strength."

16. The Silence They Count On

I was just a child, soft and small,
Believing the world was kind to all.
Taught to respect, to never defy,
To greet with a smile, never ask why.

A cousin's hug that held too tight,
A teacher's gaze that didn't feel right.
A neighbor's hand that brushed my skin,
A touch that burned deep within.

They smiled, they laughed, they played their part,
Monsters wrapped in gentle hearts.
"Don't make a scene, it's all in your head,"
But my skin still crawled from words they said.

"Shh, don't tell, who would believe?
They'll say it's you who was naïve.
You sat too close, you stayed too late,
Now hush, my dear, accept your fate."

So I learned to smile, to act the same,
To swallow the guilt, to carry the shame.
I sat at dinners with hollowed eyes,
Faking laughter, hiding cries.

I walked the streets with keys in hand,
Watched my back, rehearsed my stand.
Because the world had taught me well,
That monsters don't just live in hell.

They are uncles and fathers, brothers and friends,
The ones we trust, the ones who pretend.
And when we break, when we call them out,
The world still hesitates in doubt.

But listen now, hear me roar,
I will be silent nevermore.
This body, this voice, they both are mine,
And I refuse to walk blind this time.

To the girl who hides behind her door,
To the boy who shakes but says no more,
To the ones who thought they were alone—
You are seen. You are known.

Speak their names, take back your light,

They fear your voice—that's why they fight.
The silence they count on will end today,
Because we are louder. We will stay.

"Silence is the greatest accomplice to injustice. It's what they rely on—the hesitation, the fear, the unspoken truths that allow wrongs to go unchecked. But silence doesn't mean consent, and quiet doesn't mean weak. This poem is a reminder that your voice holds power. Even if it shakes, even if it's unheard at first—speak."

17. The Apology That Never Came

I waited—longer than I should have,
For a whisper, a word, a sign—
A fleeting moment of remorse,
That never reached this heart of mine.

I told myself, they must have tried,
That guilt must haunt their every breath.
Yet silence stood where words should be,
A graveyard filled with what was left.

Did you forget, or did you choose?
Did my tears mean so little to you?
Was my pain an inconvenience,
A truth too sharp to push through?

Nights curled up in bitter questions,
Rewriting endings in my head—
Where you stood there, eyes unshielded,
And owned the damage left unsaid.

But nothing came—no trembling voice,
No hands that shook in honest shame.
Just echoes of the love once sworn,
And the weight of your unspoken name.

Yet here I stand, no longer waiting,
No longer searching through the past.
For closure isn't found in voices,
But in knowing pain won't last.

Your silence may have built my prison,
But I hold the key within my hands.
I do not need your hollow sorrow—
I am free without your amends.

"Some wounds linger not because of what happened, but because of what never did—the apology that was owed, the closure that was denied. But waiting for words that may never come is another way of letting them win. This poem is for those who have learned to move on without the validation they deserved, finding peace in themselves rather than in an apology that will never arrive."

18. Keeping Your Girlfriends

They knew you before the world did,
Before you learned to mask and hide.
They've seen the girl behind the strength,
The cracks you carry deep inside.

From whispered notes in class back then,
To laughing loud, too wild, too free—
They knew your dreams before you spoke,
And all the things you longed to be.

They held your hand through love's first fall,
Through late-night sobs and tear-stained calls.
They hated the ones who broke your heart,
And swore they'd curse them once and for all.

They heard the lies you told yourself,
The ones that love had left behind.
And still, they stayed, they called you back—
To show you you were never blind.

They took you dancing when you swore,
You'd never smile or love again.
They made you laugh till breath was short,
And helped you heal the hurt of men.

Then life, as always, pulled its thread,
Scattered you across the map.
Jobs and love, new cities, homes—
But never once did distance last.

Because when you meet, it's still the same,
A single hug dissolves the years.
No awkward starts, no walls to break,
Just love that time could never clear.

They are the ones who just get you,
Who see the you the world does not.
No need to ask, no need to say,
Just showing up is all they've got.

So treasure them, these souls so rare,
The ones who stand through every bend.
Life may change, but let it know—
A true girlfriend stays till the end.

*"Love isn't just in grand gestures or poetic confessions.
It's in the everyday effort, the respect, the small things*

that say, "I choose you, every single day." Too often, people think winning someone's heart is the hard part— but love isn't just about finding the right person, it's about choosing them, respecting them, and growing with them."

19. The Roads Not Taken

I board the plane and take my seat,
A window view, the sky so sweet.
But in my mind, I walk the aisle,
Wings on my chest, a practiced smile.
I dreamt of flying, of skies so wide,
Yet here I sit, just along for the ride.

I hear the captain's steady voice,
A life I once saw as my choice.
Turbulence shakes, my heart does too,
Not from fear, but déjà vu.
A younger me, eyes full of light,
Wanted to chase the endless height.

I switch the channel, the match is on,
A stadium roars, the floodlights dawn.
I grip the bat—I feel the thrill,
But only in dreams, not on the field.
A kid once stood with bat in hand,
Yet fate had drawn another plan.

The hours I spent in sun and rain,
Practicing swings again and again.
Dad once cheered from the old backyard,
Said, "One day, son, you'll hit it far."
But studies called, and life was stern,
And so I watched the game, not learned.

A brush, a canvas left untouched,
A song unsung, a stage uncrushed.
A love I never dared to chase,
A moment lost, a time, a place.
The words I held, the steps untaken,
Echo in nights when I'm awakened.

I see a girl with paint-stained hands,
Creating worlds from her commands.
And I recall, so long ago,
When art had set my soul aglow.
But colors faded, pencils fell,
Dreams replaced by office bells.

A letter written, never sent,
A love confessed, then re-absent.
A call ignored, a train not caught,
A war I should have—but never—fought.
Would she have stayed, if I had tried?

Or was she meant to leave my side?

Would I have soared, would I have shined?
Or lost my way, left dreams behind?
Would I have smiled, or longed for more,
If I had walked a different shore?
Would the stars have burned a little brighter,
Or would the burdens have felt much lighter?

But roads not taken, dreams denied,
They shape the heart, they test the stride.
And though they whisper, soft yet loud,
I walk ahead, head unbowed.
For every door that stayed unopened,
Built the path that I have chosen.

"Every choice we make shapes our journey, but it's the roads we didn't take that often haunt us the most. What if I had chosen differently? What if I had been braver? What if I had fought harder? The weight of these "what ifs" is something we all carry, wondering about the lives we might have lived. But perhaps, instead of regret, we should honor those choices—they shaped the person we are today."

20. The Debt I Never Owed

You held the door, and I held my breath,
You paid for coffee—now I'm drowning in debt.
Not in coins, not in gold, not in things you could see,
But in whispers that tell me I now owe a piece of me.

A dinner, a gift, a hand when I fell,
Each kindness a contract, signed under my shell.
I didn't agree, I didn't say yes,
Yet my mind keeps running the numbers, obsessed.

I've been taught that the world keeps a ledger so tight,
That debts must be settled by the end of the night.
A favor returned, a kindness repaid,
Or else, in the balance, my worth will be weighed.

It's not that I think you'd ever demand,
It's the ghosts of the past that still hold my hand.
Too many smiles that came with a price,
Too many gestures that weren't just nice.

So I sit here, wrestling a battle unseen,
Trying to learn what trust really means.
To take without tally, to breathe and believe,
That not all who give are planning to leave.

But the weight still lingers, the fear still stays,
That kindness is currency in some cruel game.
And I wonder if ever, I'll quiet my mind,
And accept without owing, for once in my life.

A coffee offered, a bill waved away,
A friend who insists, "It's my turn today."
I smile, I nod, but inside there's a weight,
A silent debt I can't negate.

A gift unexpected, a ride back home,
A gesture so simple, yet I feel I owe.
As if kindness is currency, tallying scores,
A game where my balance is never restored.

I've traced it back to lessons ingrained,
That nothing is given without being repaid.
"Be grateful, be mindful, don't take too much,"
Yet the burden of owing feels cold to the touch.

A dinner paid for—now I keep track,
A favor extended—I plan to give back.

Not out of love, nor kindness returned,
But a fear that generosity must be earned.

But the weight still lingers, the fear still grows,
That kindness has strings only the giver knows.
Will there come a day when I finally see,
That not every hand is a chain on me?

"Not every kindness comes with a price, yet some of us have been conditioned to believe otherwise. A simple gesture—a gift, a favor, an act of care—can feel like an unspoken contract, an obligation we never agreed to. This poem is for those who struggle with the weight of unseen expectations, who battle the uneasy feeling of needing to repay what was given freely. But love, kindness, and generosity should not come with a tally. Sometimes, the hardest thing to accept is that we are worthy of receiving—without owing anything in return"

21. The Weight of Her Silence

They called her selfish, they called her cold,
For walking away from a love grown old.
"How could you leave?" they whispered low,
"A woman endures, you should know."

She left a man who barely tried,
Who drowned her voice, who clipped her pride.
Yet they asked, "Did you fight enough?"
Never him—just her, "Was love not tough?"

The vows she took, the dreams she spun,
Were buried beneath the weight of one.
One who never saw her cries,
One who fed her love with lies.

When she said, "I can't stay this way,"
They sighed and shook their heads in dismay.
"You tear the family apart for what?"
For peace, for dignity—things they forgot.

If she stayed, they'd call her weak,
"A woman should fight, not seek to leave."
If she left, she'd bear the shame,
Because it's always her to blame.

No one asked if he had strayed,
No one saw the games he played.
His absences, his bitter tone,
The way he left her all alone.

And so she carried silent pain,
A war inside, without a name.
But silence doesn't mean she's lost,
She knows now what her heart should cost.

Love is more than just the fight,
It's trust, respect, a shared light.
And if she walks, she walks for good,
Not to be praised—just understood.

She's today's girl, she makes her way,
No shame in choosing not to stay.
She writes her story, loud and clear—
"My life is mine, my heart sincere."

"Silence is not always emptiness; sometimes, it is the

loudest response. It carries stories untold, battles fought alone, and emotions too deep to name. The world often mistakes quiet for weakness, but silence can be a form of survival, of resistance, of power. This poem is for those who have been misunderstood, for those whose silence speaks volumes—because sometimes, saying nothing says everything."

22. A Stranger's Kindness

I missed my flight, the day felt cursed,
Wallet light, luck at its worst.
Staring at food I couldn't afford,
A stranger paid—"No worries, it's yours."

The streets were dark, the roads were bare,
My feet ached, but who would care?
Then headlights slowed, a window rolled—
"Hop in, kid, it's freezing cold."

The suitcase tore, my papers flew,
Crowds rushed by, like people do.
But wrinkled hands, with time so slow,
Helped me gather what I let go.

At the café, drowning in thoughts,
A waitress saw the battles I fought.
She slipped a note with my bill that day—
"You are loved, more than you say."

A train was packed, my body swayed,
Too tired to stand, but I had no say.
Then a woman smiled, rose from her place—
"Sit, dear, I've had my rest today."

We chase big dreams, seek grand applause,
But kindness lives in smaller cause.
No names exchanged, no debts remain,
Just warmth that lingers—like sweet, soft rain.

"Sometimes, the smallest acts leave the biggest impact. A stranger's smile, a helping hand, an unexpected moment of warmth—these fleeting gestures remind us that kindness is still alive in the world. And maybe, just maybe, those moments arrive when we need them the most, proving that even in a world that often feels harsh, humanity still shines through."

23. More Than What You See

*"Where are you from?"—not just my town,
But searching for what sets me down.
"You don't look Indian, are you sure?"
As if my roots must be pure.
"Your skin is dark, but pretty still,"
A backhanded praise, a bitter pill.

A name too foreign for your tongue,
A song unsung, a story shunned.
A girl denied a temple's grace,
A boy refused his rightful place.
A caste, a creed, a faith, a line,
As if a label makes us divine.

"You don't belong, you don't fit in,"
"Your people steal," "Your kind's a sin."
They build their walls with whispered fear,
Forgetting we all shed the same tear.
A scarf, a cross, a thread, a bead—

None of them change the blood we bleed.

A boy who loves a boy in shame,
A girl who fears to say her name.
A child who hides behind a lie,
Afraid to meet their father's eye.
"You'll grow out of it, it's just a phase,"
Yet their love is real in countless ways.

"Marry your own, don't cross the line."
"Lighten your skin, you'll look divine."
"Change your tongue, don't speak so loud."
"Pray like us, and you'll be proud."
A hundred ways to tear apart,
What never needed to be scarred.

We are more than what you weigh,
More than colors, love, or sway.
More than labels, more than fears,
More than scars from all these years.
We laugh, we cry, we dream, we bleed,
We are human—just like you indeed.

So stop the stares, the whispered word,
The jokes you think are never heard.
We breathe, we break, we heal, we try,
We are the same beneath the sky.

"We are all more than the labels placed upon us, more than the assumptions made at first glance. The world often rushes to define us by what's visible—our skin, our shape, our job, our past—without ever seeing the depth within. But beneath every surface lies a story, a struggle, a truth that no one can fully grasp just by looking. This poem is a reminder that every person you meet is more than what you see—just like you are, too."

24. The Burden of Being the Eldest

I came first, the chosen one,
Before my childhood had begun.
Not just a child, but built to be
The strength they'd one day need from me.

I learned to share, to step aside,
To swallow dreams and tuck my pride.
A younger hand reached out for more,
While mine just knocked on a closed door.

"I want that toy!"—but no, not mine,
"You're the eldest, wait in line."
"I want to cry!"—but dry your tears,
"You must be strong, cast off your fears."

I wanted to play, to run, to be free,
But someone was watching, looking at me.
"Behave yourself, don't break the rule,
Your sibling follows—you're their school."

So I grew up wise, I grew up fast,
I learned that my needs should come in last.
I watched them bend where I stood tall,
Their stumbles met with no scold at all.

Their "no" was softer, their "yes" more sure,
Their world was wider, their path more pure.
Not their fault—this, I knew—
But still, I longed for what they outgrew.

I was the test, the rough draft made,
The lesson learned, the toll unpaid.
I had to lead, I had to win,
No room for faults, no chance for sin.

But I loved them still, through all the ache,
Through all the things I couldn't take.
For every dream I set aside,
I saw them bloom, and swelled with pride.

Would I trade places? No, not quite,
But still, alone, on some cold night,
I whisper to the child in me—
"It's okay, now... you're finally free."

"To be the eldest is to be both a child and a parent, to

grow up too soon yet never quite be seen as grown. It means carrying responsibilities you never signed up for, watching as the younger ones are given the childhood you weren't allowed to have. And yet, you do it—not for recognition, not for praise, but out of love. This poem is for every eldest child who learned strength before they learned freedom."

25. Breaking Generational Curses

I was born into stories that weren't mine,
Handed down like heirlooms through bloodlines.
Not in gold, not in land—
But in silence, in sacrifice, in unseen hands.

"Don't dream too big," they used to say,
"Life is duty, not a child's play."
"A daughter must bend, a son must not break,"
"A family's honor is at stake."

I watched my mother swallow her pain,
Her name lost in my father's name.
Her hands built a home, her heart held the fire,
Yet no one asked what she desired.

I saw my father wear his frown,
A tired man who never sat down.
Worked his youth into aching bones,
Yet love was something he'd never shown.

"Men don't cry," they told him young,
So he buried his grief beneath his tongue.
A father who gave, but never knew—
That love is not just what you do.

And I? I was meant to fall in line,
To follow the script, to not ask why.
To inherit their fears, their silent goodbyes,
To let my dreams be compromise.

But I refuse to wear their chains,
To pass down loss wrapped up in pain.
I will rewrite what love should be,
Not a cage—but something free.

I will speak the words they never could,
Let my children be understood.
No guilt, no shame, no debts unpaid,
No love that's earned—just love that stays.

I break the curse, I start anew,
For them, for me—for those who never knew,
That love is not a war to win,
But a place where we begin.

"Generations before us did what they had to, with what they knew. Some wounds weren't their fault—but healing is our choice. To love differently, to break cycles, to be the first in the family to say, this ends with me."